Southern Living
at HOME®

Beautiful

c o n t a i n e r s

Beautiful
containers

Southern Living At HOME® Beautiful Containers
©2006 by Oxmoor House, Inc.
Book Division of Southern Progress Corporation
P.O. Box 2262, Birmingham, Alabama 35201-2262

Created exclusively for *Southern Living At HOME*,
the Direct Selling Company of Southern Progress Corporation

For information about *Southern Living At HOME,* please write to:
Consultant Support
P.O. Box 830951
Birmingham, Alabama 35283-0951

ISBN: 0-8487-3134-4
Printed in the United States of America
First Printing 2006

Many products featured in this book are from current and
previous *Southern Living At HOME* catalogs. Current products
are available for purchase.

Oxmoor House, Inc.
Editor in Chief: Nancy Fitzpatrick Wyatt
Executive Editor: Susan Carlisle Payne
Copy Chief: Allison Long Lowery

Southern Living At HOME
Senior Vice President and Executive Director: Dianne Mooney
Director of Brand Management: Gary Wright
Director of Design: Melanie Grant
Research Manager: Jon Williams

Southern Living At HOME Beautiful Containers
Editor: Rebecca Brennan
Senior Copy Editor: L. Amanda Owens
Editorial Assistant: Julie Boston
Senior Designer: Melissa Jones Clark
Photography Director: Jim Bathie
Photographers: Ralph Anderson, Robbie Caponetto,
    Mary Margaret Chambliss, Van Chaplin, Tina Cornett,
    William Dickey, Laurey W. Glenn, Brit Huckabay, John O'Hagan,
    Charles E. Walton IV
Photo Stylists: Lisa Powell Bailey, Kay E. Clarke, Buffy Hargett,
    Alan Henderson
Writers: Julia Hamilton, Kate D. Karam, Amy Bickers Mercer,
    Ellen Ruoff Riley, Shannon Sliter Satterwhite
Director of Production: Laura Lockhart
Senior Production Manager: Greg Amason
Production Manager: Tamara Nall
Production Assistant: Faye Porter Bonner

Contributors
Photographer: Jean M. Allsopp
Photo Stylists: Bob Gager, Kappi Hamilton, Susan Huff,
    Ashley Johnson Wyatt
Writers: Becky Brackenhamer, Alicia K. Clavell, Mary Leigh Fitts,
    Sarah Kinbar, Mary Katherine Pappas, Lucas Whittington
Editorial Intern: Jill Baughman

addie

welcome

Looking for creative new ways to decorate? Seeking simple and chic solutions for organization? Longing to uniquely present gifts to family and friends, as well as serve with style at your next gathering? To accomplish all this and more, look no further!

The wonderfully different shapes and sizes of ordinary containers lend themselves to extraordinary uses, from decorating to organizing to gift giving and serving. Discover how to turn even the most basic vases, bowls, and pots into fetching, functional

pieces that brighten your home, enliven your garden, and add charm to gifts. In only a few easy steps and with minimal supplies, you can transform a baking dish into a petite garden or convert pastry tins into a clever centerpiece display.

Beautiful Containers is filled with over 120 exciting ideas from the editors of *Southern Living* Books. The volume features sensational products from *Southern Living At HOME,* as well as everyday containers you probably already have on hand. Gorgeous photographs offer inspiration, often showing a variety of containers used in a multitude of practical yet eye-catching ways. After all, with the right containers, the creative possibilities are limitless!

Rebecca Brennan

Rebecca Brennan
Editor, *Southern Living* Books

decorating

Accessorizing is one of the delights of decorating. And the beauty of this pleasing pastime is that it's a quick and inexpensive way to change the mood of an entire room. Turn the page for dozens of creative ideas for using containers to express your style.

first

Invest in beautiful containers to use outdoors, and you'll always be just minutes away from having fresh, seasonal displays. Make it easy on yourself by arranging potted plants in urns; then when you're ready to change the look, all you have to do is lift out the pots and replace them with new plants. Complement the urn arrangements with a flower-filled wall bucket. Fill the bucket with moistened florist foam placed in a zip-top freezer bag to prevent leakage. Stick flower stems into the foam for a colorful decoration that lasts for days. The urn and wall bucket pairing works as beautifully at a front door as it does at a garden gate.

impressions

welcoming

Extend a warm greeting at the front door. Embellish the door with a bucket of blooms. Fill the bucket with moistened florist foam placed in a zip-top freezer bag; arrange flowers by sticking the stems into the foam. Select large plant stands as the starting point for easy-to-change seasonal decorations. Use bright mums for autumn, stately conifers for winter, blooming bulbs for spring, and elegant ferns for summer. For a special occasion, frame the door with a grapevine garland from a local crafts store. Insert flower stems into florist water vials, or use dried or permanent materials; then tuck the vials or stems into the grapevine.

style

all

Add a little magic to pots of ornamental kale by inter-twining strands of lights among the leaves. Start with 3 terra-cotta pots (8-, 12-, and 16-inch). Fill the largest pot ⅔ full with potting soil. Place the medium-size pot in the center of the larger pot; fill with potting soil as above. Center the smallest pot in the medium-size pot; fill with potting soil as above. Plant kales in all pots to fill, adding soil as needed. Water well.

a-twinkle

To add sparkle to each pot of kale, tuck battery-operated lights among the plants' leaves, hiding the battery pack among the plants.

Ornamental kale plants grow best in full sun to light shade, and they flourish in cool weather. Water daily or as needed to keep them fresh.

mantels

With the right containers in place, you'll look forward to redecorating your mantel **several times a year.** Start with a symmetrical setup—one of the easiest designs to implement. Place a tall container at each end of the mantel, and set smaller items in the center. The proportions pictured here—vertical containers paired with horizontal ones—create a pleasing traditional arrangement. Fill the tall containers with a mix of dried and permanent materials for texture and color. For special occasions, substitute fresh flowers or greenery clippings. Adorn the small center containers with petite floral bouquets and votive candles.

made easy

beachy

Sure, clear decorative containers are perfect for holding bouquets of cut flowers and seashell collections—but what about fish? A large hurricane vase makes a dandy fishbowl and sets a cheery tone for a fresh-as-all-outdoors mantel decoration. Enhance the theme by accessorizing with such coastal colors as blue and green. Add raffia ties around pillar candles to conjure images of sea grass swaying in the breeze.

keen

center stage

Create a scene at dinner with this surprisingly easy centerpiece. You'll need 4 florist-foam blocks; a hurricane vase; a low container, such as a tray or bowl; long florist picks; sheet moss; assorted flowers; and a pillar candle. Place 2 florist-foam blocks side by side on a work surface. Center the vase on top of the foam, and press gently to leave an imprint. Using a knife, cut out a square 1" around the imprint. Soak all 4 florist-foam blocks in water for 30 minutes. Assemble the arrangement as shown below.

Line the container with plastic. Place the 2 uncut florist-foam blocks side by side in the bottom of the container, and center the square you cut earlier on top, securing with long florist picks.

Cover the top tier with a layer of sheet moss, and secure with florist picks. Set the vase on the top tier, and insert florist picks at an angle around the base to secure. Place a candle in the vase. Stick stems of flowers into the florist foam, completely covering the foam.

light show

Fill drinking glasses and clear glass bowls with water, flowers, and floating candles, and arrange them along the center of the dining table to add instant elegance to a setting. Add to the tabletop fun by wrapping strips of beeswax around rolled napkins. Press the ends of the beeswax strips together, and finish with silky ties. Feel free to mix wineglasses, Champagne flutes, martini glasses, and water goblets to enjoy a variety of heights and shapes. Sprinkle clear or colored glass baubles in the bottom of each glass, and then fill the glass halfway with water to support a floating candle or flower.

asian

Let containers inspire a party theme. Here, lavender Chinese take-out boxes hold party favors and double as place markers. Pump up the color scheme by wrapping square vases with handmade paper or sturdy wrapping paper. Fill each vase with water, and top with a floating candle.

accent

infinite

Use a clear glass bowl for an endless array of creative possibilities. Fill the container with decorative rocks, marbles, fruits, or coffee beans. Top off your design with a variety of materials, such as feathers, more fruits, pinecones, flowers, and candles.

instant

Adding luscious plants nestled in handsome containers is the easiest way to bring sophisticated accents to a room. Go with compact plants, such as African violets, if a low profile is desired. Where you need height, consider using topiaries. (Place drainage trays underneath the pots, or remove the potted plants from their decorative containers before watering.) Tuck small plants into the soil, or cover the tops of the pots with moss.

effect

singular

An olive jar is a wonderful multipurpose container that can stand alone as a beautiful focal point. Filled with tall stalks of flowers and tied with raffia, it's a festive table accent. For a tabletop still life, snuggle a block of moistened florist foam in the opening of a jar and stick in stems of grapes and herbs. Use florist picks to secure such richly textured vegetables as artichokes and cauliflower to the arrangement.

sensation

casual

Elegant hurricane vases are a decorating dream. Accent one with a pillar candle and a handful of glass marbles to create singular drama. Scoop sand into a duo of large vases to anchor long-stemmed palm fronds for an intriguing, textured effect. Punctuate the arrangement with votive holders filled with candles and flowers. Vary the sizes and heights of the votive holders for an interesting interplay. This versatile display works as a grace note on a sideboard or mantel or as a centerpiece on a table.

style

branch out

Bare tree branches glued in a container filled with florist foam provide a striking backdrop for petite bouquets. You'll need a sturdy container, florist foam, a low-temperature glue gun and glue sticks, bare tree branches, sheet moss, vase ornaments, and flowers.

Using a knife, cut a piece of dry florist foam to fit snuggly inside a heavy container, such as an urn.

Apply glue to the tip of each dry, bare tree branch, and insert it into the florist foam; then add more glue around the base of the branch, and let dry. This arrangement features 6 branches.

Glue dry sheet moss to cover the foam. Fill vase ornaments or lightweight bottles with water and stems of flowers, and hang from the branches.

masterpiece
Only you'll know how easily this design comes together. You'll need a round, bubble-shaped vase; about 10 pussy willow stems; and 2 types of tulips (the long-stemmed French variety and standard lengths).

in minutes

Bend a few willow branches around the perimeter of the bowl, and then fill in the center with more branches. Cross and wind the branches over each other to form a gridlike dome.

Add water halfway up the vase. Position the tulips as desired; arrange the standard-length blooms close to the opening, and then place the longer French stems throughout for height. Fill the vase to the top with water, and add ¼ teaspoon liquid bleach to keep the water clear. The arrangement will last for about a week.

stacked for

For this showstopping display, all you need are 4 containers and 4 blooms. Fill each of 3 clear glass bowls with 1 inch of water, place a gardenia bloom inside each, and then stack the bowls. (Look for similar bowls at crafts stores.) To the side, place a hydrangea bloom in a tall vase; conceal the stem with broad leaves, such as cast-iron plant leaves. (Leaves decay faster underwater, but this arrangement will keep for a few days.)

impact

J. NEEL REID, ARCHITECT   MITCHELL   THE

GIOVANNA SCIRÈ NEPI

TREASURES OF VENETIAN PAINTI

balls of

Add interest to a clear glass container by filling it with florist-foam balls covered with mums. Start small with 2-inch florist-foam balls (when covered with flowers, they appear almost twice that size). Soak the foam balls in a mixture of water and flower food diluted according to the label directions. Cut each flower stem short, about 1 inch under the bloom head. Push stems into the foam balls, with flowers touching or overlapping, to cover the spheres entirely.

blooms

fresh and fun

Fabulous arrangements happen when fresh botanicals and imagination meet. Submerge entire blooms in vases filled with water. Add plants, fruits, leaves, and floating candles to the mix. Anchor the pieces with strands of glass beads or cuttings of chinaberries. When placed underwater, the textural beauty of such plants as bean sprouts and Boston lettuce is revealed. Look for vases in a variety of shapes to accommodate a diversity of materials. You'll never need to water these arrangements, which stay vibrant and beautiful for several days.

just add water

For a no-fuss arrangement in minutes, fill a container with water and add flowers. Dunk the blooms, or float them on the water's surface for a fun twist. Submerge shells in containers for a summery look and to help hide stems.

easy as pie

Tiny pastry tins make elegant little containers for individual flower heads. Place the tins on a tray or platter, and then add water and blooms. Use different sizes of tins and flowers for a visually pleasing arrangement.

paper wraps

Give a quick custom look to a vase of flowers. Place a vase in the center of a sheet of wrapping paper that complements the colors of your bouquet. Gather the paper in folds around the neck of the vase, and tie the paper in place with strands of raffia or a piece of ribbon. Add water and flowers. Use several arrangements along the length of the dining table, and then let guests take them home as reminders of a lovely time shared.

organizing

Use multitask containers to control clutter in stylish ways. How about a cake stand to organize shower supplies or a baking dish to tidy up a desk? On the following pages, you'll find these ideas and so many more to restore order to the daily grind.

serene

Your bathroom will be a tranquil oasis when you tuck soaps, sponges, towels, and toothbrushes into creative containers. Use baskets to hold extra washcloths and toiletries for guests. Call glass bowls into service on a sleek shelf to hold small items, such as cotton swabs, brushes, or makeup. Count on an elegant drinking glass as a chic holder for makeup brushes and cotton balls.

scene

practical

A tiered serving piece, cake stand, or footed compote take organizing to new heights. Use such a piece to keep lotions and potions within easy reach or to create a still-life vignette of hand towels and scented soaps. To enhance the ambience in a guest bathroom, add a votive holder filled with fresh blooms for a welcoming touch.

and pretty

task baskets

Woven baskets make even mundane organizing stylish. For a different approach, remove the doors from the linen closet and line the shelves with large, sturdy baskets. A rolling hamper underneath the shelves holds the dirty work, keeping outward appearances neat and tidy. Lined baskets attached to metal bars with leather straps keep towels and toiletries handy. Baskets with framed labels are smart-looking accents for dividing materials for recycling.

metal based

When it comes to order control, metal planters and vases are worth their weight in gold.
Their solid structure and well-defined lines pronounce a snappy sense of readiness. Pair planters on a
desktop, using one for function (to keep magazines and mail close at hand) and the other for form (to add
a hint of nature). Take advantage of a tall container to tame rolls of gift wrap in a most attractive way.

working

Even office supplies can become decorative accessories when neatly arranged in a clever container. Consider a similar use in the bathroom, filling the glass jars with cotton balls and swabs, hairpins, and barrettes. And, of course, a piece such as this is always on standby to trade pens and pencils for flowers and candles to become the center of attention on the dining table or mantel.

order

a tall order

Look to small shelf units or plant stands to answer the call to order. As an added bonus, the shapes of such pieces lend sculptural impact to a room. Use baskets or bowls to collect a motley mix of items, or go for an artsy look with an arrangement of pottery or china.

neatly

With a touch of imagination and a few select containers, kitchen clutter can be corralled into apple-pie order. Here, a pleasingly chunky piece of pottery and tole-painted pots rise to the challenge of making tidy work of rounding up a bevy of utensils.

useful

easy

Food bowls aren't just for serving. Pull colorful pottery baking dishes and serving bowls from the kitchen cupboard, and use them to keep such household items as pens, pencils, scissors, and glue within reach. A charming trio keeps notions right at hand alongside the sewing machine. To unify an assortment of small bowls, place them on a tray or large plate.

access

ready for

Beach supplies can quickly cause clutter chaos.
Let fanciful containers come to the rescue. Multiple
pots in a stand collect small items; larger pieces keep
such essentials as flip-flops ready to grab on the way
out the door.

action

tabletop

Use a tiered stand to transform a tabletop into a handy potting bench.
Stack pots, garden tools, gloves, and sundry materials on the shelves for an
artful and useful display. Or line up small glass jars and bowls on a multilevel
piece to create a versatile organizer in the laundry room, sewing room, or nursery.
Also try storing jars of cooking spices in the kitchen or grooming products in
the bathroom.

gardening

gift giving

Hardworking and well-designed containers have a multitude of uses. Though ideal for decorating and organizing, perhaps one of the best multipurpose uses for containers is gift giving—they're present and container all in one!

easy wraps

Give gifts that are double delights. Use decorative canisters as easy wraps that are actually gifts as well. Fill each container with several small presents—or one big one, such as this stuffed bunny—for a fun presentation. Add a bow, and the wrapping's complete!

sharing

Keep beach memories fresh by capturing a bit of sand and sea in a beautiful vase. Tuck a favorite photo into the vase, and secure it with a scoop of sand and some shells. Nestle a pillar candle into a tall hurricane vase decorated with sand and shells. Tie on a gift tag with strands of raffia for a terrific beach house hostess gift.

summer

gift fare

Look to bakeware for containers that really cook! To create a petite garden, choose a coordinating rectangular baking dish and stoneware bowl. Keep in mind that cookware doesn't have drainage holes, so select plants that don't require much water. Pour about 2 inches of aquarium gravel or small pebbles into the baking dish; insert 2 or 3 small potted succulents into the gravel at one end. Place the stoneware bowl next to the succulents. Add 1 inch of aquarium gravel to the bowl, set a potted lady's slipper on top, and then fill in with decorative rocks. Your gift's recipient can later remove the plants and use the cookware for baking. Fill a pretty baking dish with items that share a common theme, such as apples and cider mix, for a gift that's suitable for a variety of occasions.

floral favors

Turn a large glass bowl into a centerpiece that holds individual bouquet party favors. The flowers not only brighten your dinner table, but also bring joy to your guests when taken home as reminders of a pleasant evening. You'll need long-stemmed flowers; large, flat leaves, such as aspidistra; twine; gift tags; and a large bowl or glass vase.

Gather several stems of flowers, and surround the flowers with large leaves. Fold down the top of each leaf to the outside of the arrangement.

Tie the arrangement together with twine. Repeat to make a bouquet for each guest.

Using a knife, cut each bouquet to a suitable height for the container. Tie a gift tag to each bouquet, and tuck it up inside the leaves so that it won't get wet. Arrange the bouquets in a water-filled container, and place on the dinner table. Hand guests individual bouquets as they head out the door.

sundae

Add extra cheer at your next luncheon with parfaitlike flower arrangements. Sundae glasses work perfectly as vases for these dessert-themed gifts. To make a faux parfait, you'll need florist-foam powder, a glass, leaves, and flowers. For each color, combine approximately 1 cup florist-foam powder with about ½ cup water in a separate bowl. Allow the florist-foam powder to absorb moisture gradually until it sinks, and then stir well. Add more powder and water alternately until the mixture reaches the consistency of stiff mashed potatoes. Spoon the first layer of foam into a glass, and press the mixture with a spoon; repeat to fill the glass with additional layers. Insert leaves and flowers, and slowly add water to fill.

school

Float the foam powder on water, and let it absorb moisture gradually until it sinks. (Oasis Rainbow Foam is available from a florist or online at www.floraldesigninstitute.com.) Using an ice pick, pierce holes in the foam for the flower stems; keep the stems long enough to reach water as the foam dries. Replenish water often.

shimmering

The next time you give someone a bouquet, add a personal touch by decorating the vase yourself. Using easy-to-find art supplies, paint a vase to match the recipient's favorite flower or to coordinate with a room. It's easy to create a vase that's as beautiful as the blooms it contains. Using a china marking pencil, lightly outline circles, stripes, or other uncomplicated shapes on the vase. Fill in the shapes with glass paint, and let dry completely; use a rag to rub off any visible pencil lines. Curl sheer ribbon, and tie it to the neck of your vase. Add water and a colorful bouquet.

and sheer

growing

Everyone loves a present that just keeps on giving. A decorative container of bulbs continues to remind the recipient of your thoughtfulness as time goes by. Select a glass box with a lid, place a layer of pebbles in the bottom of the container, and set a few paperwhite bulbs on the pebbles. Replace the top, and tie a ribbon around the box. Include a note to keep the water level even with the base of the bulbs. Blooms will appear in about 4 to 6 weeks. Dress up terra-cotta pots with coats of paint. Plant a miniature garden of herbs or small bulbs, such as crocus, in each; fill in with tiny blooms, such as bellflowers. Tie small picture frames to florist picks, using ribbon; stick a frame into each pot as a name tag.

gifts

a trifle

Instead of taking a dessert to a party, why not fill a trifle container with something your hosts will enjoy long after the celebration is over? Glass containers with lids, such as trifle dishes and apothecary jars, can hold an assortment of small plants, making it easy for you to share your favorites. Fill the bottom of the glass container with about 1 inch of gravel; sprinkle crushed aquarium charcoal on top. (These items are available at pet stores.) Add moist potting soil. Remove plants from their pots, and loosen the roots with your fingers. Position plants snugly; then add a layer of green sheet moss or more gravel. Place the container where plants will receive diffused light. Do not overwater; use a kitchen baster to add small amounts of moisture when the soil is dry. Try these plants for small container gardens: baby's tears, ferns, peperomias, 'Petite' peace lilies, rex begonias, and succulents.

terrarium

tiny garden

Delight a gardener with a tiny oasis that fits in the palm of a hand. You'll need a 4-inch, clear glass ornament with a fitted lid and moisture-loving, small-leafed perennials (such as wintergreen, *peperomia caperata,* polka-dot plants, or most ivies) to ensure the success of the terrarium. Because it recycles its moisture, a closed terrarium can go a month or more without watering. Remind the recipient of your gift that water should be added around the bases of the plants only as needed, when the soil appears dry and crusty.

Pour about 1 inch of small gravel (available at pet stores) through a homemade funnel into the globe to help with soil drainage and to elevate the plantings.

Fill the globe with potting mix about ⅓ full. (Too much soil and moisture eventually leads to rot.) The best soil mixture contains equal parts vermiculite, perlite, and builders' sand, but nonfertilized potting soil also works.

Gently lower rooted plants into the globe, using chopsticks or long-handled tweezers. Add a few drops of water around each plant with an eyedropper. Attach the lid to the globe, and watch as condensation appears inside the globe.

serving

Whether you're setting a table for a dinner party or arranging snacks for hungry kids, everything looks more inviting served with a touch of imagination. On the following pages, you'll find fresh and unexpected ways to use common containers as stylish serving pieces.

service

Explore your attic to discover unique objects waiting to be reinvented. A chandelier base or iron tray makes a handy platter for appetizers or after-school snacks. Line the container with cloth napkins, and surround a pot of colorful blooms with a variety of clear glass containers filled with vegetables, fruits, or other goodies. Place a footed dish in the center of the piece to provide a second tier to hold bowls of dip and salsa.

with style

clearly tasteful

Clear glass bowls showcase party treats—and when the bowls are an unusual shape, they add dimension to your serving table. Consider using a stand to tier your containers so you can serve more food in a small space and lend additional aesthetic appeal. Even simple cuisine—such as colorful condiments or fresh berries—looks spectacular when given a chance to shine.

pretty on

Heighten the appeal of any serving setup with a raised container. Whether you're serving a cake or snacks—or simply looking for a smart way to present cloth napkins—you'll set a creative table with a pedestal. The extra height you gain with any footed serving piece adds a fetching dimension to the tabletop. If you don't have a pedestal in your cabinet, place a plate atop an upside-down drinking glass or bowl.

a pedestal

topsy-turvy

For a distinctive way to serve appetizers at your next function, put the platter away and flip over a footed cake stand. Any footed compote or cake stand with a hollow pedestal works. For a double-duty centerpiece and serving piece, place a small bouquet in the inverted pedestal and then surround it with fruits, cheese, and crackers. Or fill the hollow pedestal with tall breadsticks and circle it with fresh veggies for a colorful edible centerpiece. The pedestal base is also a convenient holder for appetizer skewers.

presentation

chill out

Forget that unsightly ice chest for serving frosty beverages. Most large containers can be drafted to keep bottled drinks cool. Consider a copper or galvanized bucket or washtub, or use an oversize punch bowl. You can also try a wheelbarrow for a clever portable drinks cart. To prevent drips, line the container with a plastic trash bag before adding ice.

metal works

An ironwork plant holder is a beautiful stand-in for a traditional breadbasket. Be sure to line the container with napkins; then tuck in warm muffins. Containers with intricate details make food presentation even more inviting. To style a fanciful fruit centerpiece, bunch up a cloth napkin in a metal plant holder and set an apple or grapefruit on top of the napkin. Surround the fruit base with bunches of grapes. Spear berries and cut pieces of your favorite fruits onto wooden skewers of varying lengths. Then stick each skewer into the base, and push to secure. Complete this luscious centerpiece with delicious chocolate and yogurt dips.

service on

Enliven a spring fling with funky garden pots. Roll up individual place settings of plastic flatware with paper napkins, and secure with brightly colored raffia. Place bundles into a garden pot, and set the pot on your buffet or serving table for easy access. Place a bottle of Champagne or white wine into another pot, and surround with ice to chill; or simply use it to hold a floral table decoration.

the dot

spot some fun

Line a pot with tea towels, and use it to serve brownies and cookies. Or surprise your friends by making edible "dirt" for dessert: Inside a large, clean ceramic pot (or in several if you're expecting a crowd), layer crumbled brownies and pudding as if making a trifle. Finish with a layer of pudding, and sprinkle crushed chocolate cookies on top. Insert a faux flower into the pudding, and complete the look with gummy worms. Use a clean garden trowel or plastic beach shovel to serve—and dig in!

wee ones

There's something undeniably appealing about a tiny container. Play off its inherent charm when arranging a buffet or setting the dinner table; use multiple small bowls to reinforce the look. Instead of laying vegetable dippers flat on a large platter, arrange them vertically in several small containers placed along the buffet. The upright design adds a whimsical twist to the overall setup.

small servings

To unify petite serving pieces, group them on a tray or platter. Then take advantage of having several containers at your disposal by filling some with mini bouquets and votive candles and others with condiments and edibles.

shining

Clear glass vases not only make wonderful homes for flowers, but also are terrific containers for serving. Layer flatware at an angle in a square vase to create an elegant presentation. Consider filling another vase with after-dinner mints for a coordinated look.

through

terrific

Glass tumblers make iced tea seem even more refreshing on a sweltering day. But you can also use them to serve up bunches of seasonal blossoms for guests to take home after a casual spring dinner. Embellish a party table with tumblers filled with appetizers, breadsticks, or candies.

tumblers

skewered fun

If you're seeking a classy new way to serve punch, look no further than a hurricane vase.
Prepare your favorite citrusy party drink, and let it chill. Create long, decorative strips of lemon and
lime rind with a citrus stripper. Thread lemons and limes onto wooden skewers. Layer the bottom of
the vase with maraschino cherries for an extra burst of color, and add the chilled punch. Drape strips
of rind over the edge of the vase, and set the lemon-lime skewers inside at an angle. Then grab a
ladle, and you're ready to serve this impressive beverage! Experiment with different fruits and flavors.

your name here

Use unique glasses to create one-of-a-kind place settings for guests. Wrap flatware in pretty linen napkins, and secure with ribbons. Insert the bundles into the glasses; then fluff and arrange the napkins until satisfied with the look. Tuck colorful cutouts announcing guests' names into the napkins. Place each arrangement atop a plate on the table.

stylish

Look through glassware for funky table embellishments. Spoon individual portions of party mix into small glasses, and let guests help themselves to individual snack servings. For customized place settings, convert stemmed glasses into snazzy name-card holders. Sprinkle colored sea salt, sugar, sprinkles, or candies into flutes with hollow stems. Make name cards by hand or with a computer. Thread cards onto skewers, chopsticks, or stirrers; then anchor them into the flutes.

stems

d o g s

decorating · organizing · gift giving · serving